Optimizing Your SharePoint 2013 Environments

STEVEN MANN

Optimizing Your SharePoint 2013 Environments

Copyright © 2013 by Steven Mann

Trademarks

Screenshots of Microsoft Products and Services

Warning and Disclaimer

Table of Contents

This page intentionally blank

Introduction

SharePoint 2013 is very robust and powerful. All of this robustness and power comes with a price: resources. If you have twenty available servers and can scale-out like crazy, you shouldn't have any problems. However, most of us don't have that many servers at our disposal; especially for QA and development environments.

Therefore, it is important to tweak and configure SharePoint 2013 such that you get the performance and functionality without utilizing too many resources.

This book explores various areas and options within SharePoint that may be modified, throttled, and/or disabled such that minimal resource usage is achieved in both Development/QA environments as well as Production.

Stay updated with my blog posts: www.SteveTheManMann.com

Reference links and source code is available on www.stevethemanmann.com:

This page intentionally blank

## CHAPTER 1

Web Application App Pools

Web Application App Pool Overview

When you specify a new app pool for web applications in Share-Point, an application pool is created in IIS. Each application pool results in an IIS Worker Process:

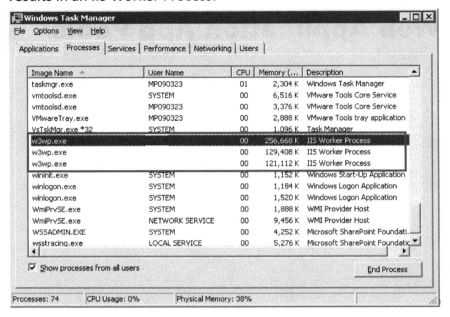

Each worker process takes up memory and CPU resources. Therefore, the more worker processes, the more resources are being used. Sharing application pools may be advantageous to reducing overall memory consumption.

Initial Web Applications

Before you create any web applications, the installation of Share-Point creates the Central Administration web application and site. Along with this is an IIS (App Pool) although SharePoint stores information about this app pool as well. This app pool should be dedicated to Central Admin

When you create other web applications, you get to choose whether to create a new app pool or use an existing one. Creating the main SharePoint web application produces an IIS Web Site on Port 80 by default and creates a SharePoint - 80 application pool accordingly.

Creating Additional Web Applications

Since most application pools are storing similar information and take up lots of memory, you may easily share app pools between web applications to reduce the consumption of resources.

DEV/QA

When creating a new SharePoint Web Application, instead of creating a new application pool, select an existing one:

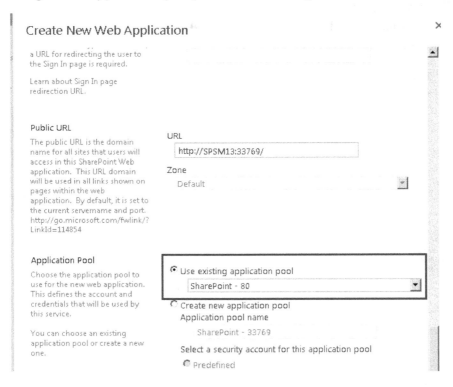

Production

You may do the same thing in Production only if you know the additional web applications will not be very large. If multiple web applications are very large in size, the application pool may take on too much memory and then decide to automatically recycle. This can be an ongoing occurrence if the shared app pool is always large.

Combining Existing App Pools

If you already have your environment built out, you may combine web applications such that they use the same app pool. Doing this via IIS does not allow SharePoint to control it and any new web front ends will not follow suit. Therefore, you need to use Pow-erShell to implement this correctly.

DEV/QA

In Development or QA environments, there are usually only a few people hitting the SharePoint sites and Central Admin. Therefore, if resources are low, you may easily modify your web applications such that they all use the same app pool. There is no harm in de-velopment and QA environments.

In my development environment, I wanted to modify Central Ad-min to use the same app pool as my main SharePoint web applica-tion (on port 80). Therefore, I would be combining the two separate app pools into one:

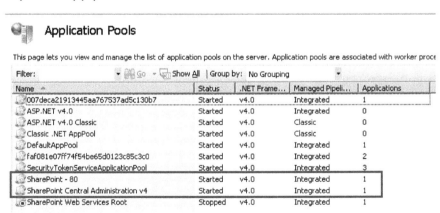

The previous state is that I have two separate application pools, one for the Central Admin web application and one for the main SharePoint web application.

Opening up SharePoint 2013 Management Shell, I can apply these commands to perform the modification:

```
# Get the source web application (main SharePoint web application on port 80)
$sourceWebApp = Get-SPWebApplication http://sp2013:80


# Get the target web application (Central Admin)
$targetWebApp = Get-SPWebApplication http://sp2013:50555


# Set the target application pool to the source application pool
$targetWebApp.ApplicationPool = $sourceWebApp.ApplicationPool


# Provision and Update
$targetWebApp.ProvisionGlobally()
$targetWebApp.Update()


# Reset IIS
iisreset
```

After performing this operation, I now only have one application pool for both Central Admin and my main SharePoint web application:

 Application Pools

This page lets you view and manage the list of application pools on the server. Application pools are associated with worker proce

Filter: Go   Show All Group by: No Grouping

Name	Status	.NET Frame...	Managed Pipeli...	Applications
007deca21913445aa767537ad5c130b7	Started	v4.0	Integrated	1
ASP.NET v4.0	Started	v4.0	Integrated	0
ASP.NET v4.0 Classic	Started	v4.0	Classic	0
Classic .NET AppPool	Started	v4.0	Classic	0
DefaultAppPool	Started	v4.0	Integrated	1
faf081e07ff74f54be65d0123c85c3c0	Started	v4.0	Integrated	2
SecurityTokenServiceApplicationPool	Started	v4.0	Integrated	3
SharePoint - 80	Started	v4.0	Integrated	2
SharePoint Central Administration v4	Started	v4.0	Integrated	0
SharePoint Web Services Root	Stopped	v4.0	Integrated	1

So now SharePoint - 80 is servicing 2 applications and the Central Admin App Pool is now servicing 0 applications. You may remove the Central Admin app pool from IIS now. SharePoint will still know about the app pool if you ever wanted to set Central Admin back. See http://stevemannspath.blogspot.com/2013/06/sharepoint-2013-listing-out-existing.html for more details.

I also have one less IIS Worker Process running and taking up memory on my development machine.

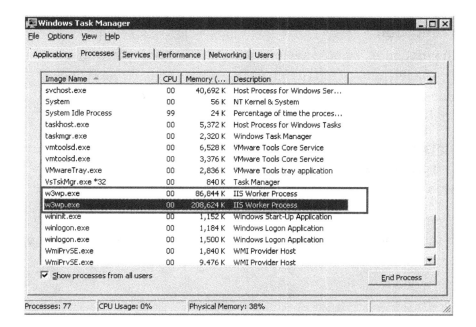

You may use the same PowerShell commands to combine other web applications so instead of using the Central Admin URL you would insert the other web application URL as the target.

Production

In Production, I would keep Central Admin and the main SharePoint web application running in separate app pools. You don't need something to go wrong and you can't get to Central Admin to fix (for example).

You could combine other web application pools but as I stated in the previous section, this all depends on the expected size of the web applications.

If anything, try to limit the amount of web applications and try to just use one web application for your SharePoint sites. This means using SharePoint - 80 to host My Sites as well.

## CHAPTER 2

Service Application App Pools

Service Application App Pool Overview

When you specify a new app pool for service applications in SharePoint, an application pool is created in IIS. Each application pool results in an IIS Worker Process:

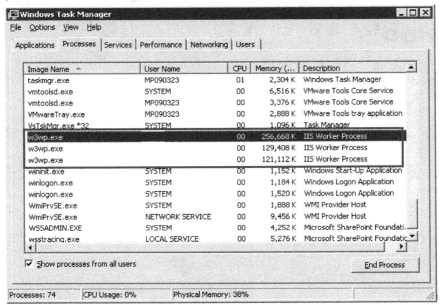

Each worker process takes up memory and CPU resources. Therefore, the more worker processes, the more resources are being used. Sharing application pools may be advantageous to reducing overall memory consumption.

Initial Creation of Service Applications

When you create service applications from the UI or from PowerShell, you can specify whether to use an existing application pool or to create a new one.

The default selection is to create a new one.

DEV/QA

For any development environment or QA environment, select the Use existing application pool option and select the out-of-the-box SharePoint application pool, "SharePoint Web Services System":

Production

Production is slightly different. While most service applications can run using the SharePoint Web Services System application pool, there are certain service applications that are recommended to use their own application pool.

The Secure Store Service is one of these, for example, because of security purposes. The Security Token Service (STS) already gets created using a separate app pool and changing this via Central Admin is not an option as the properties are disabled (and PowerShell doesn't allow it either). I would leave STS alone in Production.

Changing the Service Application App Pools

You may change the service application app pools via PowerShell or via the Central Admin UI.

PowerShell

If you going to use PowerShell to update the service application pools, you first need to know the identities (guids) of the service applications.

Run Get-SPServiceApplication in the SharePoint 2013 Management Console to list out the current service applications and their guids:

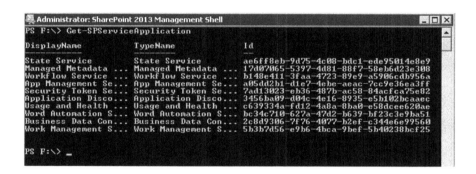

Now use those Ids for the source and targets in the following commands.

```
# Get the Source Service Application

$sourceServiceApp = Get-SPServiceApplication -Identity 17d07065-5397-4d81-88f7-58eb6d23e308

# Get the Target Service Application

$targetServiceApp = Get-SPServiceApplication -Identity 2c8d9306-7f76-4077-b2ef-c344e6e99560

# Set the Target Service Application App Pool

$targetServiceApp.ApplicationPool = $sourceServiceApp.ApplicationPool

# Update the Target Service Application

$targetServiceApp.Update()
```

Central Admin UI

This is one case where I find it easier just to change something using the UI versus PowerShell. In Central Admin, click on Manage Service Applications under Application Management:

For each service application in which you may have created a separate app pool, select it from the list and click on the Properties button from the top ribbon:

If the Properties button is disabled, then you automatically know that the app pool cannot be changed and it should be left alone.

Change the Application Pool to use the built-in SharePoint Web Services System application pool and click OK:

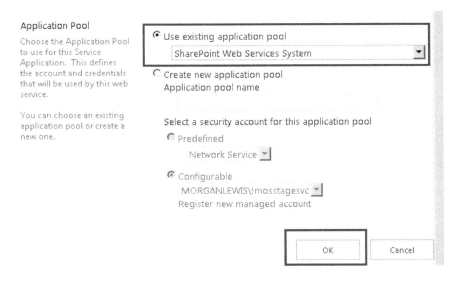

Repeat for each service application.

DEV/QA vs. Production

In development and QA environments, I would combine as many app pools as possible and have all available service applications share the SharePoint Web Services System application pool.

I already mentioned that certain service application should run within their own application pool (Secure Store Service). Therefore in Production I would create only separate app pools for these cases. Otherwise I would use the SharePoint Web Services System app pool for all others to share.

This page intentionally blank

## CHAPTER 3

Health Analyzer

SharePoint Health Analyzer Overview

The SharePoint Health Analyzer warns on various conditions that may require attention on your SharePoint farm. Many times you'll see the warning when loading Central Admin:

⊗ The SharePoint Health Analyzer has detected some critical issues that require your attention.

There are several pages of health condition rules that may or may not be applicable in all environments. Therefore, why have Share-Point do more work when it is not necessary?

DEV/QA

In development and QA environments, these health warnings will probably go ignored and only sometimes will they be resolved by the developer or QA manager. It is not production and most of the time people don't worry about these warnings.

⊿Category : Security (2)
🔖 The server farm account should not be used for other services.
🔖 Accounts used by application pools or service identities are in the local machine Administrators group.
⊿Category : Performance (2)
🔖 Databases exist on servers running SharePoint Foundation.
🔖 The paging file size should exceed the amount of physical RAM in the system.
⊿Category : Configuration (4)
🔖 Databases require upgrade or not supported.
🔖 Missing server side dependencies.
🔖 Outbound e-mail has not been configured.
🔖 Databases running in compatibility range, upgrade recommended.
⊿Category : Availability (2)
🔖 Drives are running out of free space.
🔖 Drives are at risk of running out of free space.

Rules tend to be broken in development and QA because they are not full-fledged production environments.

Therefore, if you have the time, I would go into the conditions and disable most of the rules in development and QA.

Select Monitoring from the Central Admin left navigation:

Click on the Review rule definitions link:

Click on each rule definition link you wish to disable:

Health Analyzer Rule Definitions ⓘ

⊕ new item

All Rules   •••

✓   Title

◢ Category : **Security** (4)

Accounts used by application pools or service identities are in the local machine Administrators group.

Business Data Connectivity connectors are currently enabled in a partitioned environment.

Web Applications using Claims authentication require an update.

The server farm account should not be used for other services.

Click on the Edit Item button on the top ribbon:

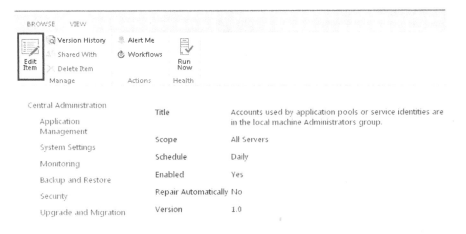

BROWSE   VIEW

Edit Item | Version History | Alert Me
Shared With | Workflows
Delete Item | Run Now
Manage | Actions | Health

Central Administration		
Application Management	Title	Accounts used by application pools or service identities are in the local machine Administrators group.
System Settings	Scope	All Servers
Monitoring	Schedule	Daily
Backup and Restore	Enabled	Yes
Security	Repair Automatically	No
Upgrade and Migration	Version	1.0

Uncheck the Enabled checkbox and click Save:

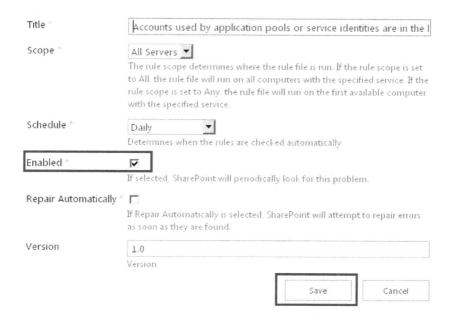

Repeat for each additional rule definition.

As an alternative, in development and QA environments, you may turn off the health analyzer all together by disabling all of the timer jobs. See the Timer Jobs chapter for more details and steps.

Production

As I stated previously, the health warnings are most likely ignored in development and QA environments, but what about production?

In production I don't want to ignore these issues but at the same time I don't want to be warned on some things that I don't need to worry about. Plus I don't need SharePoint doing more work to notify me of something that I may never change.

Before you disable anything in production, wait a week to see what kind of health warnings you receive. Review the issues and determine if they will ever be corrected or if that's just the way it is (such as some of the account rules).

Next disable the rules which fall into this case. For me, I first disabled two account rules. The reason is because some of our service accounts are used for application pools and farm accounts and may have admin privileges. It is not the recommended service account structure but it is what it is and I don't need to be notified that this is an issue; nor do I need SharePoint wasting resources trying to identify this issue and reporting it to me.

Next I disabled the Drives are at *risk* of running out of free space. Why? There is already a rule that warns of drives actually running out of disk space. I don't need to be warned about the risk. This alert was occurring against the C: drive of our servers however there is plenty of free space and since we keep our logs on the E: drive, there shouldn't be any worry. The threshold here deals with the amount of memory on the server and having enough room for logs and memory dump files. I think we are safe; you need to determine your own disk space conditions.

Finally, I changed the Database has large amounts of unused space to run Daily. I want this to be resolved on a daily basis and not have to wait for a week to realize some shrinking needs to occur (or have the amount of unused space grow even larger). I also modified this definition to repair automatically. This will shrink the database as needed.

THIS PAGE INTENTIONALLY
BLANK

## CHAPTER 4

Diagnostic Logging

Diagnostic Logging Overview

SharePoint uses the Unified Logging System (ULS) to produce logs of various events and actions that are executed, errors that have occurred, critical issues, etc. The logs come in handy when attempting to diagnose problems, however, most of the time they are a waste of resources and disk space.

You may configure the diagnostic logging settings by selecting Monitoring from the Central Admin left navigation:

Central Administration

   Application
   Management

   System Settings

   Monitoring

   Backup and Restore | Track, repo
                        SharePoint

   Security

   Upgrade and Migration

   General Application
   Settings

   Apps

   Configuration Wizards

Site Contents

Under the Reporting section, click on the Configure diagnostic logging link:

The Diagnostic Logging configuration page is rendered:

Diagnostic Logging

Event Throttling

Use these settings to control the severity of events captured in the Windows event log and the trace logs. As the severity decreases, the number of events logged will increase.

You can change the settings for any single category, or for all categories. Updating all categories will lose the changes to individual categories.

Select a category

Category	Event Level	Trace Level
☐ All Categories		
☐ Access Services		
☐ Access Services 2010		
☐ Business Connectivity Services		
☐ Document Conversions		
☐ Document Management Server		
☐ eApproval		
☐ Education		
☐ Excel Services Application		
☐ InfoPath Forms Services		
☐ Office Automation Services		

DEV/QA

In development and QA environments, select All Categories and select the least critical events to None:

You don't need SharePoint to log anything unless you are debugging an issue. I would throttle this as needed, keeping your resources available for development and QA testing.

If you have a separate drive other than C: in development and QA, change the path to the log file to use the other drive. This prevents writes to the system drive. Also, change the number of days to store log files down to a low number such as 1 or 2. This will take up less disk space and keep your drives a bit cleaner. In development and QA you usually are looking for something when it happens, not several days ago. You don't need to worry about stale log files so why keep them around?

Click OK when completed to save your changes.

Production

In Production, I usually just want to worry about the worse cases unless I am trying to trace something. Therefore, on my production farm, I tend to select All Categories and then set the least critical event log item to Critical and the least critical trace log to Unexpected:

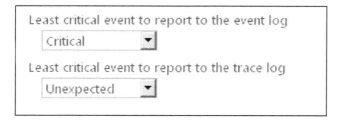

Currently, as of this writing, changing these settings may produce a ton of "Forced due to logging gap" log entries. There doesn't seem to be a workaround or fix for this as of yet but I have seen people complaining on various forums and blogs. The only way I can stop this from happening is to set everything back to the default:

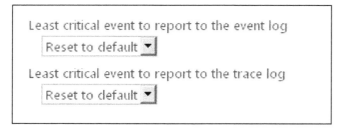

So hopefully this is corrected in a cumulative update (CU) or Service Pack.

Hopefully in Production you have an E: drive (or another drive other than C:) and can change the path of the logs to use that drive. This prevents or limits the writing to the system drive. Also, I tweak the number of days to store the log files to a lower number. In production you don't want it too low (just in case) so I changed mine to 5 days:

Path

E:\Program Files\Microsoft Office Servers\LOGS\

Example: %CommonProgramFiles%\Microsoft Shared\Web Server Extensions\15\LOGS

Number of days to store log files

5

Click OK when completed to save your changes.

## CHAPTER 5

Usage and Health Data Collection

Usage and Health Data Collection Overview

In addition to diagnostic logging, SharePoint may log events about the usage of the farm and its components/processes. While this may be helpful in analyzing usage, it is very resource and database intensive. Therefore, usage should be throttled accordingly.

DEV/QA

Unless you need to analyze something, a development SharePoint environment and any staging/QA environment should not really be doing any usage data collection:

Uncheck the option to save unnecessary resource abuse in your non-production environments. Same goes for Events to log. I have them all unchecked on my development server.

Events to log:

- ☐ Analytics Usage
- ☐ App Monitoring
- ☐ App Statistics.
- ☐ Bandwidth Monitoring
- ☐ Content Export Usage
- ☐ Content Import Usage
- ☐ Definition of usage fields for Education telemetry
- ☐ Definition of usage fields for service calls
- ☐ Definition of usage fields for SPDistributedCache calls
- ☐ Definition of usage fields for workflow telemetry
- ☐ Feature Use
- ☐ File IO
- ☐ Page Requests
- ☐ REST and Client API Action Usage
- ☐ REST and Client API Request Usage
- ☐ Sandbox Request Resource Measures
- ☐ Sandbox Requests
- ☐ SQL Exceptions Usage
- ☐ SQL IO Usage
- ☐ SQL Latency Usage
- ☐ Task Use
- ☐ Tenant Logging
- ☐ Timer Jobs
- ☐ User Profile ActiveDirectory Import Usage

You may also uncheck the Enable health data collection option as well:

☐ Enable health data collection

Click the link below to edit the health logging schedule.
   Health Logging Schedule

Production

Production is a bit different. You may want to track usage of your SharePoint farm. If this is the case, enable usage data collection:

> ☑ Enable usage data collection

However, only log the events that you truly care about tracking:

Events to log:
- ☐ Analytics Usage
- ☐ App Monitoring
- ☑ App Statistics.
- ☐ Bandwidth Monitoring
- ☐ Content Export Usage
- ☐ Content Import Usage
- ☐ Definition of usage fields for Education telemetry
- ☐ Definition of usage fields for service calls
- ☐ Definition of usage fields for SPDistributedCache calls
- ☐ Definition of usage fields for workflow telemetry
- ☑ Feature Use
- ☐ File IO
- ☑ Page Requests
- ☐ REST and Client API Action Usage

Again, it is also a good idea to keep the logs on a separate drive to reduce the writes on the C: system drive:

Log file location:

E:\UsageLogs

Health data collection is good to run in production so you may be forewarned of any issues:

☑ Enable health data collection

Click the link below to edit the health logging schedule.
Health Logging Schedule

Clicking on the Health Logging Schedule allows you to tweak the timer job frequencies. For the most part they run Daily or Hourly and seem to be pretty well behaved. I would leave these alone and worry about disabling the jobs that aren't necessary (see the Timer Jobs chapter).

## CHAPTER 6

Timer Jobs

Timer Jobs Overview

Timer jobs are scheduled processes that perform various functions to keep SharePoint running smoothly. These jobs are run by the SharePoint Timer Service which is constantly running on the SharePoint farm servers:

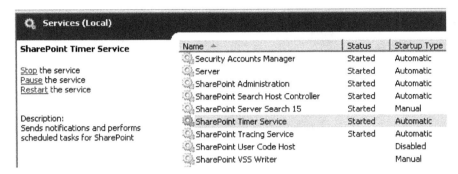

The service program is OWSTIMER.EXE:

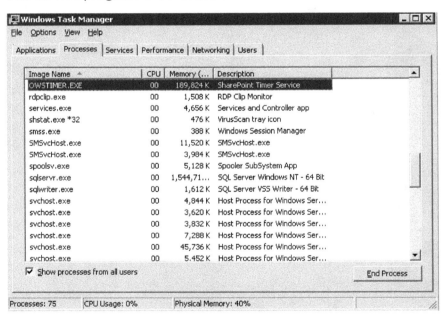

It is constantly running and does take up some memory, however, you can reduce the amount of work it needs to perform by tweaking the timer jobs that need to run.

To do this, first select Monitoring from the Central Admin left navigation:

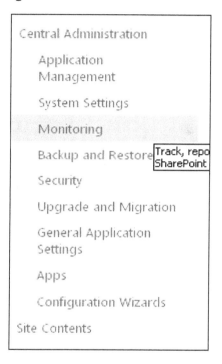

Under the Timer Jobs section, click on the Review job definitions link:

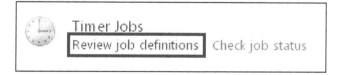

On the Job Definitions page, select each timer job definition you want to disable:

Job Definitions

Title

Analytics Event Store Retention

App Installation Service

App State Update

Application Addresses Refresh Job

Application Server Administration Service Timer Job

Application Server Timer Job

Audit Log Trimming

Autohosted app instance counter

Bulk workflow task processing

CEIP Data Collection

Cell Storage Data Cleanup Timer Job

Change Log

Content Organizer Processing

Content Type Hub

On the Edit Timer Job page, click the Disable button to disable the timer job:

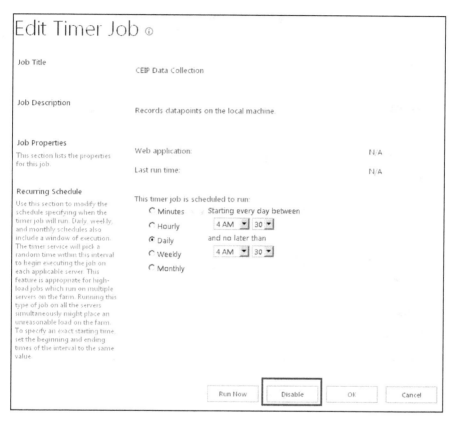

The Timer Job is now disabled:

Audit Log Trimming	SharePoint - 80	Monthly
Autohosted app instance counter		Weekly
Bulk workflow task processing	SharePoint - 80	Daily
CEIP Data Collection		Disabled
Cell Storage Data Cleanup Timer Job	SharePoint - 80	Daily
Change Log	SharePoint - 80	Weekly

Timer Jobs to Disable

The Timer Jobs that you should disable deal with the services or features that you are not using in any environment. Therefore the ones to choose in development, QA, and production all depend on the answer to the question, "Am I using this feature?"

Some jobs may already be disabled based on your tweaking of the Diagnostic Logging, Health Collection, and Usage settings. So besides those, here are the timer jobs that stand out as questionable:

CEIP Data Collection: Are you participating in the Customer Experience Information Program? No? Disable

eDiscovery In-Place Processing: Are you using the eDiscovery services in SharePoint? No? Disable

Education Bulk Operation: Are you using the Education Services? No? Disable

{I think I am going to create a guide on the Education Services - stay tuned}

Holds Processing and Reporting: Are you using holds anywhere?

SharePoint Server CEIP Data Collection: Are you again participating in the Customer Experience Information Program?

Variations jobs (multiple): Are you using variations anywhere in SharePoint?

Most jobs that need to run, execute in seconds if not milliseconds. So disabling these only makes a small difference in memory and performance. The overall feeling here is that the less SharePoint has to do, the better it can perform the things it needs to do.

## CHAPTER 7

Services on Server

This chapter is designed mainly to bring your attention to services that may be running on Production servers that do not need to be running. In a Development or QA/Staging environment, where servers are limited (if not singular), you may not be able to stop or remove these services.

Services on Server Overview

The Services on Server may be accessed via Central Admin by clicking the Manage services on server link under System Settings:

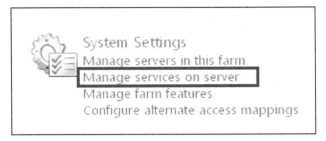

This brings up the Services on Server page:

Services on Server ⊙

| | Server: | spsm13 ▾ | View: | Configurable ▾ |

Service	Status	Action
Access Database Service 2010	Stopped	Start
Access Services	Stopped	Start
App Management Service	Started	Stop
Business Data Connectivity Service	Stopped	Start
Central Administration	Started	Stop
Claims to Windows Token Service	Stopped	Start
Distributed Cache	Started	Stop
Document Conversions Launcher Service	Stopped	Start
Document Conversions Load Balancer Service	Stopped	Start
Excel Calculation Services	Stopped	Start
Lotus Notes Connector	Stopped	Start
Machine Translation Service	Stopped	Start

This page displays all of the main SharePoint services (which mostly correlate to Service Applications but not all) that may be stopped or started on the selected server.

By using the Server drop-down, you may navigate to each server in the current farm by changing the server:

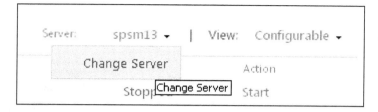

For best reference on which services should run on each server, check out the Plan Service Deployment article on TechNet (http://technet.microsoft.com/en-us/library/jj219591.aspx)

The key takeaway here is to make sure that you aren't bogging down your servers with services that shouldn't be running on them.

Microsoft SharePoint Foundation Web Application

When you install SharePoint on any server, the installation assumes that it is going to be a web front end. Therefore the IIS web sites and all of the web application goodness (services) are installed and processes are fired up and started.

So this means that even when you are configuring an application server, the web sites are copied over and installed. This means that application pools are running and IIS Worker Processes are taking up memory and CPU.

Therefore, after installing and configuring an application server (including dedicated Search servers), you can stop the Microsoft SharePoint Web Application service:

Microsoft SharePoint Foundation Sandboxed Code Service	Stopped	Start
Microsoft SharePoint Foundation Subscription Settings Service	Stopped	Start
Microsoft SharePoint Foundation Web Application	Started	Stop
Microsoft SharePoint Foundation Workflow Timer Service	Started	Stop
PerformancePoint Service	Stopped	Start
PowerPoint Conversion Service	Stopped	Start

Since this is configured to run on all web servers, many people forget that it doesn't need to run on the non-web-front-end servers.

Microsoft SharePoint Foundation Workflow Timer Service

The SharePoint Foundation Workflow Timer Service is also configured to run on all web servers so it is installed and fired up after installation. Again, this service does not need to run on the application servers - so it can be stopped on any non-web-front-end server as well:

Microsoft SharePoint Foundation Incoming E-Mail	Stopped	Start
Microsoft SharePoint Foundation Sandboxed Code Service	Stopped	Start
Microsoft SharePoint Foundation Subscription Settings Service	Stopped	Start
Microsoft SharePoint Foundation Web Application	Started	Stop
Microsoft SharePoint Foundation Workflow Timer Service	Started	Stop
PerformancePoint Service	Stopped	Start

Claims to Windows Token Service

The Claims to Windows Token Service (C2WTS) only needs to run on servers that run the Excel Services service and/or PerformancePoint Services. The TechNet documentation also states that it needs to run on any server running a service application that needs to pass SharePoint identities to external data sources.

While additional configuration is required for SQL Server 2012 and accessing external data, the C2WTS doesn't need to run on all of your servers in the farm.

Distributed Cache

By default the Distributed Cache is installed and started on every installation. Not only does the Distributed Cache service not need to run on every server, you will get warned if it is running on too many servers in the farm. In fact, with this "bad-boy", not only should it be stopped but also removed from the servers that it does not need to run.

Essentially this service should run only on the web front end servers unless you have a Distributed Cache and Request management tier. Then it should only run on the servers participating in the Distributed Cache and Request management tier and not the web front end servers.

To remove this service from the servers that do not need them, you need to run the following PowerShell commands on each server separately:

```
Stop-SPDistributedCacheServiceInstance -Graceful
Remove-SPDistributedCacheServiceInstance
```

## CHAPTER 8

IIS Web Logs

Web Logs Overview

SharePoint web applications run under IIS, so of course, regardless of SharePoint, IIS itself produces logs of any web access.

Logging in IIS is configured at each web site. Selecting a web site, such as the SharePoint - 80 web application and then clicking Logging in the main window opens the Logging dialog.

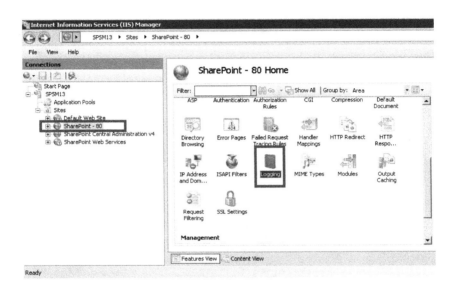

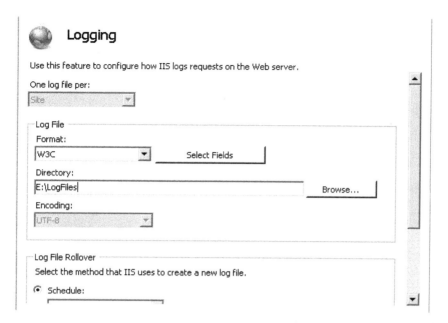

Logging

Use this feature to configure how IIS logs requests on the Web server.

One log file per:

Site

Log File

Format:

W3C   Select Fields

Directory:

E:\LogFiles   Browse...

Encoding:

UTF-8

Log File Rollover

Select the method that IIS uses to create a new log file.

Schedule:

No matter what environment, switching the location of the log files to a drive other than C:, reduces disk writes to the system drive.

DEV/QA

In development and QA/Staging environments, there really is no reason to have IIS pounding away at the log files. You already have SharePoint doing its fair share of using disk resources. Therefore, there is no harm in disabling the IIS logging for all web applications on these servers.

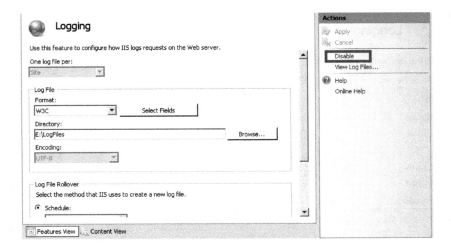

Production

If you are not using the IIS logs for access analysis and tracking in production, I would disable the IIS logging for each web application in IIS.

CHAPTER 9

Central Admin Web Site

Central Admin Web Site Overview

By default, the Central Administration web site is created on the C: drive using the default inetpub web site location. Many times administrators would like all of the web sites to run on a different drive, such as E:, since C: is a System Drive. While creating Web Applications, you may specify the location; the creation of Central Admin does not give you that option. You can easily move Central Admin to a different drive following the simple steps in this chapter.

Moving the web site to a different drive reduces disk activity on the system drive (C:). I move Central Admin to E: in all of my environments. Overall there is probably not much to be gained but since I create the web applications on E:, having all of the virtual directories in one place makes things more manageable.

Moving the Central Admin Web Site

Step 1: Navigate to the SharePoint Central Administration and select Manage Web Applications

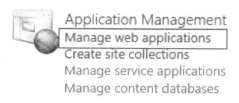

Application Management
Manage web applications
Create site collections
Manage service applications
Manage content databases

Step 2: Select the Current SharePoint Central Administration web application

Name

SharePoint - 80

SharePoint Central Administration v4

Step 3: Extend the Web Application

From the Web Applications top ribbon menu, click on the Extend button:

BROWSE   WEB APPLICATIONS

New Extend Delete General Settings Manage Features Managed Paths Service Connections

Contribute   Manage

Step 4: Specify the Port and Location

This is where you specify the new non-C-drive location.

Step 5: Verify the URL and the Zone

Click OK.

Step 6: Remove SharePoint from IIS Web Site

You aren't really deleting the web application but back on the Manage Web Applications page, with the SharePoint Central Administration web application selected, you need to click on Delete button menu from the top ribbon:

Select Remove SharePoint from IIS Web Site:

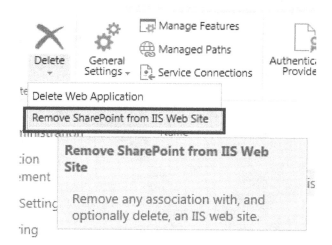

Step 7: Select the Original Central Admin Web Site

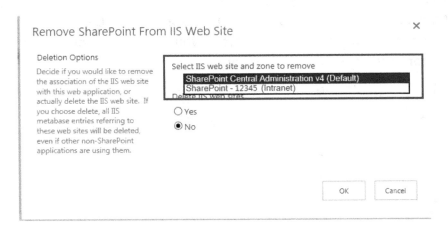

In the Remove SharePoint From IIS Web Site dialog, make sure the original Central Admin web application name is selected. Make sure Delete IIS Web Sites is set to Yes. Click OK.

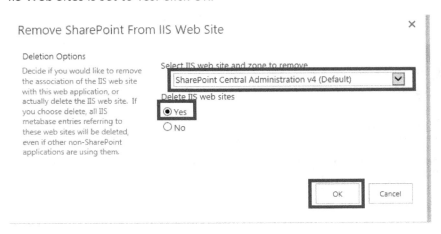

Since you are removing the IIS site (and port) from which you are currently administrating SharePoint, you will receive an error:

This page can't be displayed

- Make sure the web address http://dvvsp01:26897 is correct.
- Look for the page with your search engine.
- Refresh the page in a few minutes.

This means that the old site is down and now Central Admin is running on the new port that you specified during the extending process.

Step 8: Run the SharePoint 2013 Products Configuration Wizard

The SharePoint 2013 Central Administration menu item won't navigate to the new location until the configuration wizard is run.

## CHAPTER 10

Request Manager

Request Manager Overview

Request Manager is a process that allows SharePoint 2013 to manage incoming requests. Request Manager may run on the web front ends of your farm but also can be used on dedicated request servers. Request Manager is facilitated by starting the Request Management Service on those servers.

At a bare minimum, starting the service on the web front ends without modifying any throttling, allows SharePoint to determine which web front end should receive the incoming request.

Here are some suggested readings on Request Management:

http://www.harbar.net/articles/sp2013rm1.aspx

http://technet.microsoft.com/en-us/library/jj712708.aspx

Implementation of Request Management

The easiest and simplest way to implement SharePoint's Request Manager is by activating the Request Management service on the web front ends. This can be performed using PowerShell or by clicking Start in Services on Server.

PowerPoint Conversion Service	Stopped	Start
Request Management	Stopped	Start
Search Host Controller Service	Started	Stop
Search Query and Site Settings Service	Started	Stop

DEV/QA

On development servers it doesn't make sense to run the Request Management service at all. Leave it in the Stopped state. For QA, if you have multiple web front ends, you may want to think about starting the service to improve performance. Most QA and/or staging environments aren't the most powerful and often times slow already. The Request Management may help a bit here.

Production

At the very least, starting the Request Management service in your production environment on each web front end will provide health -based request throttling. Your load balancer usually balances connections and requests but does not know what SharePoint is doing otherwise.

The Request Management service knows what SharePoint is doing and may decide to pass a request to a different web front end if the one that gets the request is busy with other things. The SharePoint Request Manager just may provide your farm some additional performance gains for "free".

CHAPTER 11

Content Databases

Content Database Overview

```
☐ 📁 Databases
    ☐ 📁 System Databases
    ☐ 📁 Database Snapshots
    ☐ 📄 SharePoint_AdminContent_30d91e2f-3218-47ba-b362-3f9ba95103d7
    ☐ 📄 SharePoint_Config
    ☐ 📄 SP2013_State_Service
    ☐ 📄 WSS_Content
☐ 📁 Security
☐ 📁 Server Objects
```

The Content Databases store all of the content for all of the site collections on the farm within a given web application. This includes list items, documents, web part settings, user information, and other site related configurations.

Each web application must have at least one content database but may have multiple. A site collection can only live in one content database. While the recommended max size is 200GB (although up to 1TB is supported), I personally like smaller 40-50GB content databases. It is easier to backup and restore smaller databases as well as copying the backup files around to different servers.

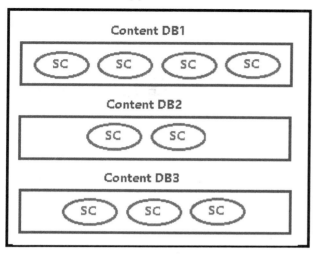

Adding Content Databases

In all environments, I like to have many content databases to spread the site collections evenly across. Smaller databases are easier to access, retrieve content, and backup/restore.

To add content databases, click on the Manage content databases link within Central Admin under Application Management.

Application Management
Manage web applications
Create site collections
Manage service applications
Manage content databases

Monitoring
Review problems and solutions
Check job status

Add or configure content databases that are attached to a web application

On the Content Databases page, click on the Add a content database link:

Content Databases ⓘ

🖮 Add a content database

Database Name	Database Status	Database Read-Only
WSS_Content	Started	No

On the Add A Content Database page select the web application and enter a new content database name:

Web Application: http://spsm13/ ▾

Database Server

devsvr

Database Name

DEV_CONTENT_2

Click OK to create the content database. It may take a few seconds to generate the new database and return to the Content Databases screen:

Content Databases ⓘ

📧 Add a content database

Database Name	Database Status	Database Read-Only	Current Number of Site Collections
DEV_CONTENT_2	Started	No	0
WSS_Content	Started	No	3

The new content database is displayed in the list.

Development

You shouldn't have to worry about the content databases in development. It all depends on how many different site collections you create. If you think you are going to create many site collections, I would create a few content databases in development - especially if you feel that SharePoint is slow on your dev box.

QA/Production

Since the QA/Staging environment should mimic your Production environment, they both should have the same content databases and thus the same content. I would have least five (5) content databases for the main SharePoint web application.

I like lean and mean content databases. I don't like to have content databases that exceed 50GB. It is easier to backup, restore, and move around smaller databases. Spreading out your content can help keep your site performance up.

About the Author

Steve Mann was born and raised in Philadelphia, Pennsylvania, where he still resides. He is an Enterprise Application Engineer for Morgan Lewis and has more than 19 years of professional experience. He has authored and co-authored several books related to collaboration technology. Steve graduated Drexel University in 1993.

Steve's blog site can be found at: www.SteveTheManMann.com

Follow Steve on Twitter @stevethemanmann

www.ingramcontent.com/pod-product-compliance
Lightning Source LLC
Chambersburg PA
CBHW061025050326

40689CB00012B/2704